More than you know...

ALL RIGHTS RESERVED

Copyright © 2023 by Mia'Bella "Lovie" Baylson

To book the Author for a book review, media appearance &/or speaking engagements, please send a request to: Loviegirl6565@gmail.com

Published By: Author Overnight Publications & Designs
www.authorovernight.info

Sent With Love To:

Today will be
a great day

Dedication

I want to thank some people that were there for
me when I needed them.

My parents:
(my mom Megan, my dad Bart, my stepmom
Beau and my stepdad Eric).
Murray, my cousin Jojo, Blake, Johanna, Joyce,
my tutor Sheila Crackenberger, my teachers, my
friends, and the rest of my family.

Thank you for everything you do & helping me
when I'm hurt or sad.

Love always,
Mia'Bella "Lovie" Baylson

"About myself"

I was 9 when I wrote this book; I hope you like it. I will probably still be 9 when this book comes out, and I want you to know that if I can do this, so can you. I know this because I believe in you.

~Mia

Write about a friend or family member you admire...

Chapter 1

The story of my life

Hello, my name is Mia'Bella Lovie Baylson. I don't like to be called Mia'Bella because my parents call me that when I'm in trouble. I like to be called Mia. Ever since I was five years old, I have always wanted to be a fashion designer when I grow up. When I see people design things, I'm like, "wow." I'm only nine, but just because I'm nine doesn't mean I should give up. I know this because three people told me to never to give up (my mom, dad, and stepmom), and I believe them. They said you can do anything you want in life if you work hard. So I'm asking you to believe it too.

What do you want to be when you grow up?

Learning to be thankful

I Live under a roof. Some people don't even have food to eat or a roof over their heads. If you believe in God, you may not, but you are blessed to have a roof over your head. There are some people out there that do not have a home. When I say my prayers at night, I say, God, I hope you help the sick and suffering and help them find a place to stay Amen. You can really pray for anything that is on your heart.
Do you have a prayer that you say?

My prayer is...

____

____

____

Today I'm grateful for...

Chapter 3

You Are Loved

Have you ever heard of someone who does not like to do homework? Well, I'm one of those someones. I don't like homework, but I know I have to do it. Do you ever think you're not good enough or seen? I have at times, and it hurts inside. Well, I want to let you know that you are enough. I would Like you to write 20 things about yourself that are positive. Here are mine, are you ready?

My Affirmations:

1. I am special

2. I am Loved

3. I am beautiful

4. I am kind

5. I am smart

6. I am encouraging

7. I am blessed

8. I am nice

9. I am amazing

10. I am helpful

11. I am enough

12. I am the best

13. I am hopeful

14. I am a good leader

15. I am sweet

16. I am bold

17. I am loving

18. I am joyful

19. I look out for others

20. I am important

Now it's your turn:

1. _______________________________
2. _______________________________
3. _______________________________
4. _______________________________
5. _______________________________
6. _______________________________
7. _______________________________
8. _______________________________
9. _______________________________
10. _______________________________
11. _______________________________
12. _______________________________
13. _______________________________
14. _______________________________
15. _______________________________
16. _______________________________
17. _______________________________
18. _______________________________
19. _______________________________
20. _______________________________

Now that you have this,
whenever you feel sad inside,
take a deep breath and read
the positive things you wrote.

No matter what happens, I
want you to know that you are
LOVED.

I love you,

~Mia'Bella Lovie Baylson

Chapter 4

Big Trouble

I did not want to share this because I was embarrassed, but my mom and my publisher said it would help a lot of people. So here it goes.

I got in trouble.

Big trouble.

I got suspended from school and was grounded in my room for 5 whole days, Thursday, Friday, Saturday, Sunday, and Monday. It was the worst punishment in my life. My parents told me I could only come out to eat. I freaked out. I cried for an hour on the phone with my mom because I hated it. I was so mad at myself. It felt like my life was over, and I would be stuck in my room forever. My mom told me to use that time and create something amazing. She told me that I was creative and could create something magical. That is when I wrote this Book.
If you're ever in trouble, it's not the end. You can create something cool or write a book like I did. You got this.

What are some things
you could create...

____

____

____

____

____

____

____

____

____

____

____

____

____

____

____

Chapter 5

You Are Magical... Let's get creative.

**This is your chance to write a story about anything at all that is in your heart. It can be about your life, your dream life, or completely make-believe.
When we use our creativity, WE CREATE MAGIC.**

**YOU ARE
Magical...**

Your story...

Your story...

Your story...

Your story...

Chapter 6

Do you like games? I love them.
This is the 5-day thank you game. For the next 5 days, you pick one person a day and write them a thank you letter or card. You can make the card and get as creative as you want. Write down every day who you picked, what you made for them, and how it made them feel.

You can get super creative.

Day 1:

Day 2:

Day 3:

Day 4:

Day 5:

Chapter 7

When I get sad at school I walk away and tell myself
3 things:

I am loved
I am kind
I am beautiful

It makes me feel better.
What are 3 things you can tell yourself if someone
ever hurts your feelings?

The three things I can tell myself are...

If I could be a superhero, I would be...

My real-life hero is, and why...

Who is one person you can help feel better tomorrow, and what can you do for them?

Tomorrow
Will be
Beautiful

What is one thing you can do today to help your mom or dad?

I would love to learn
how to...

My favorite thing to do is...

When I get older, I would like to be...

YOU ROCK

My favorite toy or video game is...

Write 3 things you like
best about your family...

My favorite part of school is...

Three things I love about myself are...

BEING NICE

IS THE COOLEST

My favorite tv show is...

My biggest fear is...

Today I feel...

I feel scared when...

START YOUR MORNING WITH A SMILE

The best subject in
school is...

The worst subject in school is...

My best friends are...

What makes me feel
happy inside...

BE BRAVE

What makes me feel feel brave and strong...

I wish I had...

The best vacation would be...

I would love it if...

____

____

____

____

____

____

____

____

____

____

____

____

____

____

____

____

YOU GOT THIS

List 5 ways you can be a good friend...

If I had 3 wishes, they would be...

If animals could talk, I would ask them...

If I were my teacher, I would...

You are not your mistakes

What is the best book you have ever read and why?

Write three sentences to describe your room...

At recess, I like to...

BE
YOU

My favorite holiday is...

Sometimes I don't understand...

I love when my parents...

YOU BELONG
YOU HAVE PURPOSE
YOU ARE A STAR

If I had a yes day, it would look like...

The first thing I will do when I become an adult is...

NEVER FORGET
YOU BELONG
YOU MATTER
YOU ARE LOVED